MW01156050

JAMS AND PRESERVES

**Text by Jacqueline Bellefontaine
and Judith Ferguson
Photography by Peter Barry
Designed by Philip Clucas**

3383
This edition published in 1993 by Tiger Books International PLC, London
© 1993 CLB Publishing Ltd, Godalming, Surrey
Printed and bound in Singapore by Tien Wah Press
All rights reserved
ISBN 1-85501-355-X

JAMS AND PRESERVES

TIGER BOOKS INTERNATIONAL
LONDON

CONTENTS

INTRODUCTION

The old fashioned art of preserving is enjoying a comeback. More and more of us are beginning to make preserves and jams, not so much as a way of preserving fruit and vegetables to enjoy all year round, but because we enjoy cooking and appreciate the flavour and texture of home-made preserves, so often superior to the commercially produced varieties.

In many ways we are luckier than our forebears, with exotic fruits and vegetables readily available in our supermarkets which we can use as well. In this book you will find recipes for truly fabulous exotic preserves and pickles – for instance paradise jam or hot pepper jelly – alongside traditional favourites.

Being home-made, these preserves have no additives to prolong their shelf life and it is wise to store jars in the refrigerator after opening. Pickles, relishes and whole preserved fruit are best stored in the refrigerator as soon as they are made.

Excellent jams and preserves can be made with the minimum of basic equipment. You will need a preserving pan or a large saucepan. This should be large enough to ensure that the ingredients do not come more than two-thirds of the way up the pan, so that a good rolling boil can be achieved without spilling over. A long wooden spoon is required to stir the jam. A jelly bag or muslin is required for some of the jellies but these are not expensive, and a funnel is useful to prevent messy potting. Of course, you will need plenty of jars, and special preserving jars are best used for bottling as they are less likely to break during the cooking process.

Pectin plays an important role in successful jam and jelly making. It is the clear, jelly-like substance found naturally that makes jams and jellies set. Apples, red and black currants, plums and citrus fruit are high in pectin, while cherries, berries, rhubarb and tropical fruits such as pawpaw are low in pectin. Our grandmothers and great-grandmothers had to mix high pectin fruits such as chopped apple to low pectin fruits in order to make jams set. Today, however, jam sugar – which is granulated sugar with powdered pectin – is readily available in the shops and can be used to make jams and jellies set, even those made from fruit juice, wine or tea. Bottled pectin is sometimes available and can also be used, following the instructions on the bottle.

Use the cooking times given as a guide only, as a number of factors will effect the time: the size of the pan or the ripeness of the fruit, for instance. You will therefore need to test for a set and many people have their own favourite way. Remember to remove the pan from the heat whilst testing for a set or the preserve may over cook and spoil. If you make a mistake and pot too early, you can return it to the pan and reboil for a few minutes. In which case, remember to wash and re-sterilize the jars.

To Test for set:
• Spoon a small amount of the jam liquid onto a cold plate. The jam should cool quickly and the surface will wrinkle when the jams is pushed with the finger.
• Spoon some of the jam onto a wooden spoon and cool quickly. If setting point is reached the jam will fall off slowly from the spoon in one large drop, if it runs off the spoon in a stream then further boiling is needed.
• For some preserves, such as the fruit butters and thick jams, a wooden spoon can be pulled through the pan and if it leaves a trail (so that you can see the base of the pan momentarily) then the setting point has been reached. Where this test is appropriate it has been suggested in the recipe.

Potting:
In order to ensure that the preserves keep well they must be poured into jars which have been sterilized first. Rinse in water and shake out the excess. Place in a warm oven for about 10 minutes. Once the jars are filled cover the surface of the preserve with a waxed disc, waxed side down, and seal.

Hopefully this book will encourage you to take up this old art and discover the truly unique flavour that only home-made preserves provide. Let it inspire you to bring it right up to date with some delicious new combinations.

Quantities of ingredients in each recipe are given in metric and imperial and it should be noted that these are not interchangeable.

PRESERVES, JAMS AND SPREADS

Ginger Pear Jam

A bright, clear and golden jam with a pleasant hint of ginger. Quick and easy to make with a high yield.

PREPARATION TIME: 20 minutes

COOKING TIME: 50 minutes

MAKES: Approximately 2.3kg/5lbs

1.8kg/4lbs firm pears
850ml/1½ pints water
60g/2oz grated fresh ginger root
Juice of 1 lemon
1.4kg/3lb sugar

Peel and core the pears, and cut them into thick slices. Place in a preserving pan with the water, ginger and lemon juice. Tie the peel and core in a square of muslin and add to the pan. Cook the pears until soft and pulpy, about 30 minutes. Remove the muslin bag. Mash the fruit or push through a sieve. Stir in the sugar and heat gently, stirring until sugar is dissolved. Boil rapidly until setting point is reached. This should take about 20 minutes. Test with a wooden spoon; if the spoon leaves a channel, setting point has been reached. Pour into hot, sterilized jars, then seal and label.

This page: Ginger Pear Jam (top) and Strawberry and Banana Jam (bottom). Facing page: Three-Fruit Marmalade (top) and Orange and Grapefruit Marmalade with Whisky (bottom).

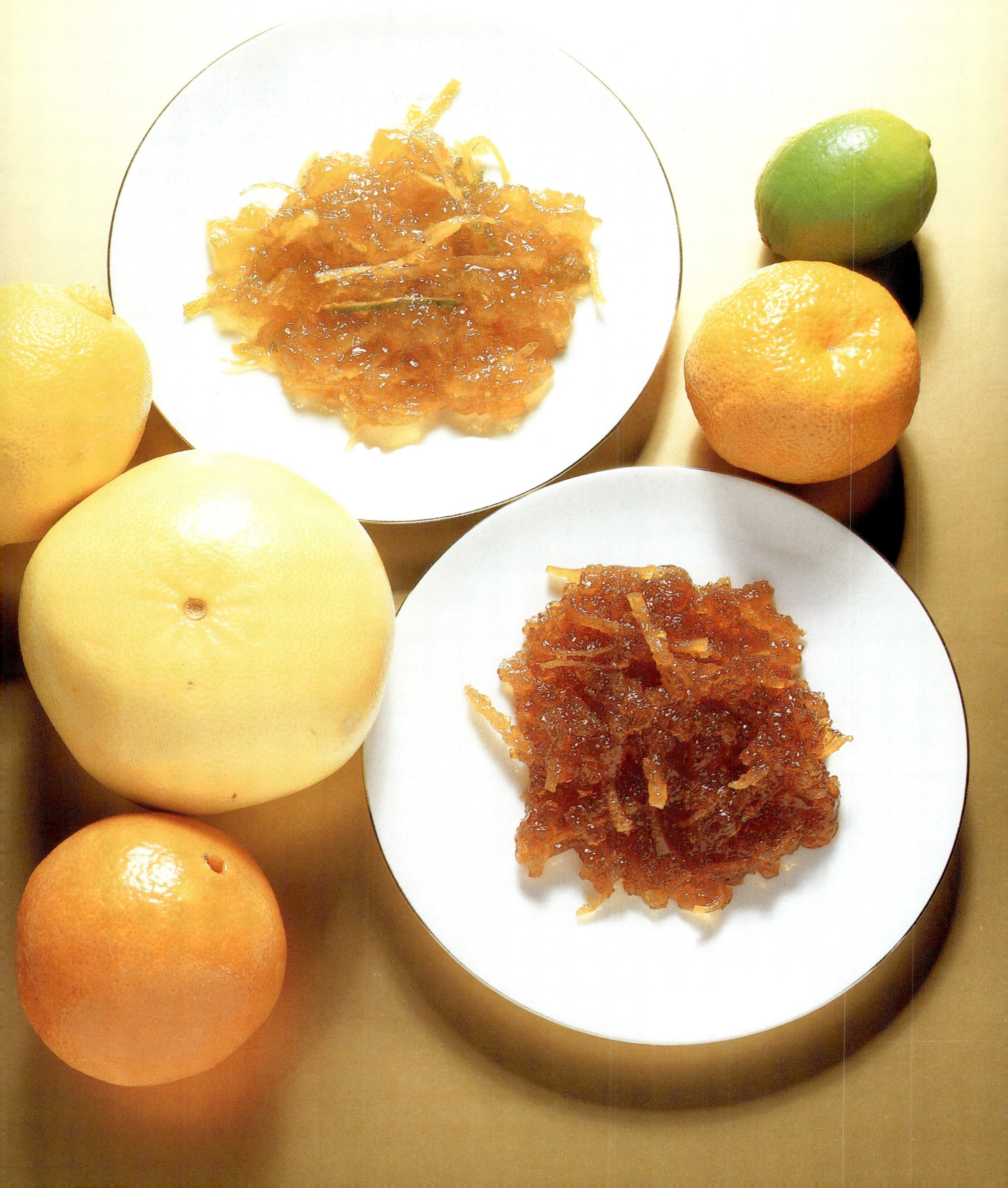

Apple and Calvados Jam

A smooth-textured jam with a delicious hint of Calvados.

PREPARATION TIME: 20 minutes

COOKING TIME: 40 minutes

MAKES: Approximately 2.5kg/5½lbs

1.8kg/4lbs cooking apples
700ml/1¼ pints water
Juice and grated rind of 1 lemon
1.4kg/3lbs sugar
140ml/¼ pint Calvados

Peel and core the apples and cut into thick slices. Place in a preserving pan with the water, lemon juice and rind. Tie the peel and core in a square of muslin and add to pan. Cook apples until soft and pulpy, about 20 minutes. Remove the muslin bag. Mash the fruit or push through a sieve. Stir in the sugar and heat gently, stirring until sugar is dissolved. Boil rapidly until setting point is reached – about 10 minutes. Test with a wooden spoon; if the spoon leaves a channel, setting point has been reached. Stir in the Calvados. Pour into hot, sterilized jars, then seal and label.

Orange and Grapefruit Marmalade with Whisky

Although the yield is not great, this tangy marmalade can be made with Seville oranges if desired.

PREPARATION TIME: 50 minutes

COOKING TIME: approximately 1½ hours

MAKES: Approximately 1.4kg/3lbs

3 oranges
3 grapefruit
1.1litres/2 pints water
675g/1½lbs light brown sugar
30g/1oz butter (if necessary)
60ml/4 tbsps whisky

Wash the fruit and pare off the coloured part of the skin with a sharp knife, taking care not to include too much of the white pith. Cut the peel into shreds and squeeze the juice from the fruit. Tie the remaining pith and seeds in a square of muslin. Put the juice, peel and muslin bag into a preserving pan with the water and simmer gently for about 1 to 1½ hours, or until the peel is soft and the contents of the pan have been reduced by about half. Remove the muslin bag and squeeze out well. Stir in the sugar and heat gently, stirring until all the sugar is dissolved. Boil rapidly without stirring until setting point is reached. If the marmalade looks bubbly and cloudy, stir the butter in to help clarify it. Stir in the whisky, then allow to stand for 20 minutes before potting. Seal and label.

Plum Nut Jam

A jam with a crunch, which makes it rather special.

PREPARATION TIME: 5 minutes

COOKING TIME: 50 minutes

MAKES: Approximately 3.2kg/7lbs

1.8kg/4lbs plums, washed
850ml/1½ pints water
45ml/3 tbsps lemon juice
1.8kg/4lbs sugar
225g/8oz roasted hazelnuts, chopped

Place the plums in a preserving pan with the water and lemon juice, and simmer gently for 30 minutes. Stir in the sugar and cook gently, stirring until all the sugar has dissolved. Stir in the hazelnuts. Boil rapidly until setting point is reached, removing the plum stones with a slotted spoon as they rise to the surface. Pour into hot, sterilized jars, then seal and label.

Plum Nut Jam (above right) and Apple and Calvados Jam (far right).

Blackberry and Apple Jam

A traditional jam with an excellent colour and reliable set.

PREPARATION TIME:	20 minutes
COOKING TIME:	40 minutes
MAKES:	Approximately 3.2kg/7lbs

1.4kg/3lbs blackberries, washed
220ml/8 fl oz water
675g/1½lbs cooking apples, peeled,
cored and chopped
2kg/4½lb sugar

Place the blackberries in a preserving pan with the water and cook gently until soft. Add the apples and continue cooking until they are soft and pulpy. Break the apples up with the back of a wooden spoon as they cook. Stir in the sugar and cook gently, stirring until all the sugar has dissolved. Boil rapidly until setting point is reached, stirring frequently. Pour into hot, sterilized jars, then seal and label.

Blueberry Jam with Cassis

A sweet jam which can be made from fresh or frozen blueberries.

PREPARATION TIME:	10 minutes
COOKING TIME:	35 minutes
MAKES:	Approximately 1.8kg/4lbs

900g/2lbs blueberries
280ml/½ pint water
45ml/3 tbsps lemon juice
900g/2lbs sugar with added pectin
60ml/4 tbsps crème de cassis
   (blackcurrant liqueur)

Place the blueberries, water and lemon juice in a preserving pan, and cook until the fruit is very soft. Stir in the sugar and cook gently, stirring until all the sugar has dissolved. Boil rapidly for 5 minutes. Remove from the heat and test for set; boil for a little longer if required. Stir in the crème de cassis. Pour into hot, sterilized jars, then seal and label.

This page: Blackberry and Apple Jam.
Facing page: Blueberry Jam with Cassis.

Strawberry and Banana Jam

A delicious variation of a favourite jam.

PREPARATION TIME:	15 minutes
COOKING TIME:	20-30 minutes
MAKES:	Approximately 1.8kg/4lbs

900g/2lbs strawberries, washed
900g/2lbs sugar with added pectin
4 large bananas
30ml/2 tbsps lemon juice

Pat the strawberries dry on a clean cloth, then slice and place in a preserving pan with the sugar. Cook over a low heat until the sugar is dissolved, stirring frequently. Peel and cut the bananas into chunks and add to the pan along with the lemon juice. Cook until bananas soften, then increase the heat and boil rapidly for 3 minutes. Test for set and boil a little longer if necessary. Pour into hot, sterilized jars, then seal and label.

Lemon Lime Curd

Delicious spread on bread or as a filling for cakes.

PREPARATION TIME: 10 minutes

COOKING TIME: 50 minutes

MAKES: Approximately 675g/1½lbs

Grated rind and juice of 2 lemons
Grated rind and juice of 1 lime
45g/1½oz unsalted butter
225g/8oz caster sugar
3 eggs, beaten

Place the rind and juice into the top of a double boiler or in a bowl placed over a pan of gently simmering water. Add the butter and cook until melted. Stir in the sugar and continue cooking until sugar has dissolved, stirring occasionally. Strain the beaten eggs into the juice mixture and cook gently until the curd thickens, stirring constantly. Take care not to over-heat the mixture or it will curdle. If the mixture does start to curdle, remove from the heat immediately and whisk rapidly. The curd is cooked when the mixture coats the back of a spoon. Pour into dry jars, then seal and label. Best stored in the refrigerator.

Chocolate, Orange and Hazelnut Spread

Quick and easy to prepare, this spread will go down well at any children's party.

PREPARATION TIME: 10 minutes

COOKING TIME: 20 minutes

MAKES: Approximately 225g/8oz

30g/1oz unsalted butter
60g/2oz sugar
Grated rind and juice of ½ orange
60g/2oz cocoa powder
15ml/1 tbsp evaporated milk
1 egg, beaten
120g/4oz ground hazelnuts

Place the butter and sugar in the top of a double boiler or in a bowl placed over a pan of gently simmering water. Cook until the butter has melted and the sugar dissolved. Stir in the orange rind, juice, cocoa and evaporated milk and mix well. Strain the egg into the mixture and cook gently until thickened slightly. Stir in the hazelnuts and cook for 5 minutes, stirring constantly. Allow to cool slightly, then pour into dry jars, seal and label. Best stored in the refrigerator.

Three Fruit Marmalade

A great marmalade to make towards the end of the year, when stocks of marmalade made from Seville oranges are getting low.

PREPARATION TIME: 45 minutes, plus 20 minutes standing time

COOKING TIME: 1½ hours

MAKES: Approximately 1.6kg/3½lbs

4 limes
4 tangerines
4 lemons
1.1litre/2 pints water
900g/2lbs sugar
30g/1oz butter (if necessary)

Wash the fruit and pare off the coloured part of the skin with a sharp knife, taking care not to include too much of the white pith. Cut the peel into shreds and squeeze the juice from the fruit. Tie the remaining pith and seeds in a square of muslin. Put the juice, peel and muslin bag into a preserving pan with the water, and simmer gently for about 1 hour, or until the peel is soft and the contents of the pan have been reduced by about half. Remove the muslin bag and squeeze out well to extract any liquid. Stir in the sugar and heat gently, stirring until all the sugar is dissolved. Boil rapidly without stirring until setting point is reached. If the marmalade looks bubbly and cloudy, stir the butter through the mixture to help clear it. Allow to stand for 20 minutes before potting. Seal and label

Rhubarb and Raspberry Jam

Raspberries are added to rhubarb to make a fabulously fruity and inexpensive jam.

PREPARATION TIME: 30 minutes, plus 20 minutes standing time

COOKING TIME: 40 minutes

MAKES: Approximately 2kg/4½lbs

675g/1½lbs rhubarb, cut into small pieces
140ml/¼ pint water
675g/1½lbs raspberries
45ml/3 tbsps lemon juice
1.4kg/3lbs sugar

Place the rhubarb with the water into a preserving pan and simmer gently for 10 minutes, or until the rhubarb is just soft. Add the raspberries and lemon juice, and continue to cook for 10 minutes, or until all the fruit is very soft. Stir in the sugar and cook gently, stirring until all the sugar has dissolved. Boil rapidly until setting point is reached. Allow to stand for 20 minutes, then stir. Pour into hot, sterilized jars, then seal and label.

Facing page: Lemon Lime Curd (top) and Chocolate, Orange and Hazelnut Spread (bottom).

stirring until the sugar is dissolved. Boil rapidly until setting point is reached. Test with a wooden spoon; if the spoon leaves a channel, setting point has been reached. Pour into hot, sterilized jars, then seal and label.

Apricot Jam

A beautiful golden jam, which always seems to have a good flavour.

PREPARATION TIME: 20 minutes

COOKING TIME: 50 minutes

MAKES: Approximately 3kg/6¾lbs

1.8kg/4lbs fresh apricots, halved and stoned
280ml/½ pint water
30ml/2 tbsps lemon juice
4 whole cloves
1.8kg/4lbs sugar

Put the apricots, water, lemon juice and cloves in a preserving pan and cook until the fruit is very soft and pulpy and the contents are reduced by about a quarter. Remove the cloves and stir in the sugar. Heat gently, stirring until sugar is dissolved. Boil rapidly until setting point is reached. Pour into hot, sterilized jars, then seal and label.

Pineapple and Coconut Jam

A good jam for children, as a topping for buns or a filling for cakes.

PREPARATION TIME: 15 minutes

COOKING TIME: 45 minutes

MAKES: Approximately 1.8kg/4lbs

1.2kg/2¼lb crushed canned pineapple, in natural juice
Juice of ½ lemon
900g/2lb sugar with added pectin
275g/10oz shredded coconut, fresh or packaged

Place all ingredients in a preserving pan and heat gently, stirring until the sugar dissolves. Make sure all the sugar is fully dissolved, or it may

Quince and Cardamom Preserve

An interesting alternative to the more familiar quince jelly.

PREPARATION TIME: 20 minutes

COOKING TIME: 45 minutes

MAKES: Approximately 1.6kg/3½lbs

1.2kg/2¼lbs quinces
1 litre/1¾ pints water
1 orange, halved lengthwise then thinly sliced crosswise
45ml/3 tbsps cardamon pods
1.4kg/3lbs sugar

This page: Pineapple and Coconut Jam (top) and Rhubarb and Raspberry Jam (bottom). Facing page: Apricot Jam (top) and Quince and Cardamom Preserve (bottom).

Peel and core the quinces, and cut them into thick slices. Place in a preserving pan with the water and orange slices. Tie the peel and core in a square of muslin and add to the pan. Cook the quince until soft and pulpy. Remove the muslin bag and squeeze out the liquid. Mash the fruit against the side of the pan. Crush the cardamoms and add the seeds to the pan. Stir in the sugar and heat gently,

crystallize. Boil gently, stirring until setting point is reached. Skim off any scum that may form. If jam leaves a channel when a wooden spoon is pulled through it, the setting point has been reached. Pour immediately into hot, sterilized jars, then seal and label.

Paradise Jam

A jam made from a selection of exotic fruits now readily available in shops.

PREPARATION TIME: 15 minutes

COOKING TIME: 40 minutes

MAKES: Approximately 1.8kg/4lbs

2 large pawpaw (papaya)
4 passion fruit
2 guava
340g/12oz canned crushed pineapple, in natural juice
About 140ml/¼ pint water
30ml/2 tbsps lime juice
1.4kg/3lbs sugar with added pectin

Peel and finely chop the papaya. Place in a preserving pan. Cut the passion fruit in half, scoop out pulp and seeds, then add to the pan. Peel and chop the guava and add to the pan. Drain the pineapple and make juice up to 240ml/9fl oz with water. Add to the pan along with the pineapple. Stir in the lime juice and cook gently until the fruit is very soft and pulpy. Stir in the sugar, then heat gently, stirring until the sugar is dissolved. Boil rapidly until setting point is reached. Pour into hot, sterilized jars, then seal and label.

Kiwi Fruit and Apple Honey

A refreshing and interesting preserve that spreads like honey.

PREPARATION TIME: 15 minutes

COOKING TIME: 50 minutes

MAKES: Approximately 1.2kg/2¼lbs

4 kiwi fruit
140ml/¼ pint water

450g/1lb sugar
450g/1lb honey
400g/14oz cooking apples, peeled, cored and finely chopped
5ml/1tsp lemon juice
Green food colouring (optional)

Peel and chop the kiwi fruit. Heat the water, sugar and honey together in a preserving pan, stirring until sugar

This page: Paradise Jam.
Facing page: Kiwi Fruit and Apple Honey.

dissolves. Add the kiwi fruit, apple and lemon and cook very gently until the preserve darkens and thickens. Stir frequently to prevent the jam from burning. Allow to cool slightly, place in a food processor and blend until smooth, with a little food

colouring. Leave to stand a few minutes to allow bubbles to disperse, then pour into hot, sterilized jars, seal and label.

Brandy Peach Jam

Only firm, unbruised peaches should be used for this luxurious jam.

PREPARATION TIME: 45 minutes

COOKING TIME: 45 minutes

MAKES: Approximately 1.8kg/4lbs

1.8kg/4lbs peaches
280ml/½ pint water
30ml/2 tbsps lemon juice
Cinnamon stick
1.4kg/3lbs sugar
140ml/¼ pint brandy

Skin peaches by plunging first into boiling water for a few moments and then into cold water. The skin should peel away easily. Slice the peaches, dicarding the stones. Put the peaches, water, lemon juice and cinnamon in a preserving pan and cook until fruit is very soft and pulpy – this should take about 20 minutes, depending on how ripe the peaches are. Remove the

This page: Whole Strawberry Preserves with Grand Marnier. Facing page: Brandy Peach Jam (top) and Autumn Jam (bottom).

cinnamon and mash with a potato masher or push through a sieve. Stir in the sugar and heat gently, stirring until sugar is dissolved. Boil gently until setting point is reached, about 25 minutes. Stir regularly as this jam will burn easily. Stir in the brandy and pour immediately into hot, sterilized jars, then seal and label.

Rose Petal and Cherry Preserve

Rose petals give this jam a lovely scented flavour, but they can be omitted.

PREPARATION TIME: 25 minutes	
COOKING TIME: 25 minutes	
MAKES: Approximately 2kg/4½lbs	

1.4kg/3lbs cherries
1.1litre/2 pints water
1.2kg/2¼lbs sugar with added pectin
2.5ml/½ tsp rose water
Handful rose petals, washed and dried

Wash and stone the cherries. Place in a preserving pan with the water. Bring to the boil, then simmer gently for 15 minutes or until the cherries are soft. Stir in the sugar and rose water and cook gently until sugar dissolves. Boil rapidly for 5 minutes, then test for a set. Boil for a few minutes longer if necessary and test again. Once setting point is reached, stir in the rose petals and pour into hot, sterilized jars. Seal and label.

Whole Strawberry Conserve with Grand Marnier

This luxury preserve makes an ideal gift for a 'foodie' friend.

PREPARATION TIME: 10 minutes, plus standing time	
COOKING TIME: 10-15 minutes	
MAKES: Approximately 2.7kg/6lbs	

1.8kg/4lb strawberries
1.8kg/4lb sugar with added pectin
60ml/4 tbsps lemon juice
60ml/4 tbsps Grand Marnier

Hull the strawberries, using only firm, unblemished berries. Wash them and leave to dry. Layer the strawberries into a preserving pan, sprinkling sugar between each layer. Set aside until the juice begins to run. Heat gently, stirring until the sugar has dissolved. Add the lemon juice, then boil rapidly for 5 minutes. Remove from the heat and test for a set, boiling for a few more minutes if necessary. Do not over-stir at this stage or the berries will break up. Stir in the Grand Marnier. Allow the jam to cool considerably, then stir to distribute the strawberries. Pot into warm, sterilised jars, then seal and label.

Autumn Jam

Make this jam with fruits that are plentiful in the autumn for a tasty jam to consume during the winter months.

PREPARATION TIME: 15 minutes	
COOKING TIME: 45 minutes	
MAKES: Approximately 1.8kg/4lbs	

450g/1lb plums, stoned
280ml/½ pint water
450g/1lb apples, peeled, cored and sliced
450g/1lb pears, peeled, cored and sliced
45ml/3 tbsps lemon juice
1.4kg/3lbs sugar

Place the plums and water into a preserving pan and cook gently for 5-10 minutes, or until the plums are soft. Add the apples, pears and lemon juice and cook for 10-15 minutes, or until the apples and pears are soft and pulpy. Stir in the sugar and heat gently, stirring until the sugar is dissolved. Boil rapidly until setting point is reached. Test by stirring with a wooden spoon; if the spoon leaves a channel, then setting point is reached. Pour into hot, sterilized jars, then seal and label.

Right: Rose Petal and Cherry Preserve.

Pineapple Grapefruit Marmalade

Pineapple and grapefruit compliment each other wonderfully in this recipe.

PREPARATION TIME: 50-60 minutes, plus standing time

COOKING TIME: 1½ hours

MAKES: Approximately 2.3kg/5lbs

2 large pineapples
3 grapefruit
570ml/1 pint water
675g/1½lbs sugar
15g/½oz butter (if necessary)

Peel and cut the pineapples into small pieces. Wash the grapefruit and pare off the coloured part of the skin with a sharp knife, taking care not to include too much of the white pith.

This page: Peach butter with Whisky (top) and Apple Butter (bottom). Facing page: Pineapple Grapefruit Marmalade (top) and Plum Butter (bottom).

Cut the peel into shreds and squeeze the juice from the fruit. Tie the remaining pith and seeds in a square of muslin. Put the juice, peel, muslin bag and pineapple into a preserving

pan with the water and simmer gently for about 1 hour, or until the peel is soft. Remove the muslin bag and squeeze out well. Stir in the sugar and heat gently, stirring until all the sugar is dissolved. Boil rapidly without stirring, until setting point is reached. If the marmalade looks bubbly and cloudy, stir the butter through the mixture to help clear it. Allow to stand for 20 minutes before potting. Seal and label.

Plum Butter

Tasting just like jam, this preserve is very smooth and creamy in texture.

PREPARATION TIME: 20-30 minutes	
COOKING TIME: 40 minutes	
MAKES: Approximately 1.4kg/3lbs	

1.4kg/3lbs plums
7.5ml/1½ tsps ground ginger
140ml/¼ pint water
675g/1½lbs sugar

475

Wash the plums, cut in half and remove the stones. Place the plums, ginger and water in a preserving pan and cook gently for 10 to 15 minutes, or until the plums are tender. Stir in the sugar and heat gently, stirring until sugar is dissolved. Boil rapidly until a wooden spoon leaves a channel when pulled through the mixture. Allow to cool slightly, then purée in a food processor until smooth. The mixture should be thick and creamy. Push through a sieve if a really smooth texture is required. Pour into hot, sterilized jars; seal and label.

Cherry and Almond Preserve

A sophisticated jam most adults adore.

PREPARATION TIME: 25 minutes	
COOKING TIME: 25 minutes	
MAKES: Approximately 2kg/4½lbs	

1.4kg/3lbs cherries
120g/4oz blanched almonds
1.1litre/2 pints water
1.2kg/2¼lbs sugar with added pectin
2.5ml/½ tsp almond essence

Wash and stone the cherries. Split the almonds in half. Place cherries and almonds in a preserving pan with the water. Bring to the boil, then simmer gently for 15 minutes, or until the cherries are soft. Stir in the sugar and cook gently until it dissolves. Boil rapidly for 5 minutes, then test for a set. Boil for a few minutes longer if necessary and test again. Once setting point has been reached, stir in the almond essence. Cool slightly, stir and pour into hot, sterilized jars. Seal and label.

Peach Butter with Whisky

A slightly wicked-tasting, fruity spread with a hint of honey.

PREPARATION TIME: 30 minutes	
COOKING TIME: 30 minutes	
MAKES: Approximately 1.4kg/3lbs	

1.4kg/3lb peaches
120ml/4 fl oz water
340g/12oz clear honey
1.25ml/¼ tsp ground cloves
2.5ml/½ tsp ground nutmeg
60ml/4 tbsps whisky

To peel the peaches, cut a small slit in the skin at the stem end and plunge into boiling water for a few seconds. Refresh in a bowl of cold water. The skin should now peel away easily. If not, plunge in boiling water for a little longer. Cut peaches in half, remove the stones and slice the fruit. Place the peach slices and the water in a preserving pan and cook gently for about 15 minutes, or until the peaches are tender. Stir in the honey, cloves and nutmeg. Cook for about 10 minutes, until a wooden spoon leaves a channel when pulled through the mixture, stirring constantly to prevent burning. Allow to cool slightly, stir in

Cherry and Almond Preserve (right).

the whisky, and purée (in batches) in a food processor until smooth. The mixture should be thick and creamy. Push through a sieve if a really smooth texture is required. Pour into hot, sterilized jars, then and seal and label.

Elderberry Jam

Gathering elderberries from the hedgerow brings back childhood memories and makes for an inexpensive jam.

PREPARATION TIME: 10 minutes	
COOKING TIME: 25 minutes	
MAKES: Approximately 1.8kg/4lbs	

1.4kg/3lbs elderberries
1 apple, peeled, cored and chopped
30ml/2 tbsps lemon juice
140ml/¼ pint water
1.2kg/2¼lbs sugar

Wash the berries and strip from the stalk. Place in a preserving pan with the apple, lemon juice and water. Cook gently for 10 minutes, or until the fruits are soft. Stir in the sugar and boil rapidly until setting point is reached. Cool slightly, stir and pour into hot, sterilized jars. Seal and label.

Grape Jam

This soft-setting jam is popular on the Continent, but less well known in England. It is delicious served with croissants.

PREPARATION TIME: 10 minutes	
COOKING TIME: 35 minutes	
MAKES: Approximately 2.7kg/6lbs	

1.4kg/3lbs black grapes
280ml/½ pint water
45ml/3 tbsps lemon juice
1.8kg/4lbs sugar

Halve the grapes and remove the pips. Place in a preserving pan with the water and lemon juice, and cook gently for 10 minutes. Stir in the sugar and when dissolved, boil rapidly until setting point is reached. Cool slightly, stir and pour into hot, sterilized jars. Seal and label.

This page: Grape Jam (top) and Elderberry Jam (bottom).

Apple Butter

A dark, creamy spread with a slightly caramelised flavour.

PREPARATION TIME: 30 minutes	
COOKING TIME: 40 minutes	
MAKES: Approximately 900g/2lbs	

1.4kg/3lbs apples such as Bramley or Granny Smiths
140ml/¼ pint unsweetened apple juice
5ml/1 tsp ground cinnamon
225g/8oz light brown sugar for every 450g/1lb fruit pulp

Cut the apples in quarters, but do not peel or remove the stems or cores. Place in a preserving pan with the apple juice and cinnamon and cook until soft and pulpy. Push the apple mixture through a sieve and discard the peel, core and stems. Weigh the apple pulp and add the required amount of sugar. Heat gently until sugar dissolves and bring to the boil. Boil gently for about 20 to 30 minutes or until the butter is thick and creamy. Stir frequently to stop it from burning on the bottom. Pour into hot, sterilized jars, then seal and label.

PRESERVED WHOLE FRUIT

Preserved Kumquats

These kumquats taste wonderfully exotic.

PREPARATION TIME: 15-20 minutes

COOKING TIME: 45-60 minutes

MAKES: Approximately 675g/1½lbs

450g/1lb whole kumquats
225g/8oz sugar
420ml/¾ pint water
45ml/3 tbsps Cointreau

Cut a cross in the top of each kumquat and pack into screw-top preserving jars. Heat sugar and water gently until sugar dissolves, then boil for 1 minute. Stir in the Cointreau. Pour in syrup to within 1cm/½-inch of the top of the jar. Screw lids on, then release a quarter turn. Place layers of folded newspaper in the bottom of a deep pan. Put the jars in and fill with warm water, up to the necks. Heat in ½ hour to simmering. Simmer for 10 minutes or until kumquats look clear. Remove the jars and immediately fully tighten lids. Label when cold and store in a cool, dark place.

Apples in Ginger Wine

Serve with whipped cream or Greek yogurt for an instant special dessert.

PREPARATION TIME: 15 minutes

COOKING TIME: 35 minutes

MAKES: Approximately 2.7kg/6lbs

420ml/¾ pint green ginger wine
420ml/¾ pint water
570g/1¼lbs sugar
1.4kg/3lbs apples, peeled, cored and sliced

Place wine, water and sugar in a

saucepan and cook gently until sugar dissolves, bring to the boil and boil for 1 minute. Pack apples into screw-top preserving jars. Pour in syrup to within 1cm/½ inch of the top of jars. Screw lids on then release a quarter

This page: Preserved Kumquats (top) and Apples in Ginger Wine (bottom).

turn. Place layers of folded newspaper in the bottom of a deep pan. Put the jars in and fill the pan with warm water up to the necks. Heat slowly in ½ hour to simmering. Simmer for 2 minutes. Turn off heat. Top up jars with any remaining hot syrup. Tighten lids and cool in the water. Label and store in a cool, dark place.

Cherries and Peaches in Kirsch

Kirsch gives extra flavour to this dessert.

PREPARATION TIME: 15 minutes	
COOKING TIME: 10 minutes	
MAKES: Approximately 1.2kg/2¼lbs	

450g/1lb peaches
225g/8oz cherries
60g/2oz whole blanched almonds
225g/8oz sugar
140ml/¼ pint water
Approximately 280ml/½ pint kirsch

Plunge peaches into boiling water for 1-2 minutes to loosen the skins. Peel, quarter and discard stones. Pack peaches, cherries and almonds into warm, sterilized jars. Heat sugar and water together slowly until sugar dissolves, bring to the boil and boil for 4 minutes. Add an equal quantity of kirsch to the syrup. Pour over fruit and seal jars. Label and store in a cool, dark place, for at least 2 weeks before using.

Brandied Apricots

These apricots are truly delicious.

PREPARATION TIME: 10 minutes	
COOKING TIME: 10 minutes	
MAKES: Approximately 1.4kg/3lbs	

900g/2lbs apricots
225g/8oz sugar
280ml/½ pint water
Cinnamon sticks
Approximately 280ml/½ pint brandy

Wash the apricots and prick several times with a needle, to help the syrup penetrate the fruit. Heat sugar and water slowly until the sugar dissolves, bring to the boil, add the apricots and simmer gently for 5 minutes. Remove apricots and pack into jars. Add half a

stick of cinnamon to each jar. Strain syrup through muslin and pour equal amounts into each jar; top up with brandy to cover the fruit completely. Seal and store in a cool, dark place for at least 2 weeks before using.

Spiced Orange Slices

These orange slices make a luxurious accompaniment for roast meats.

PREPARATION TIME: 15 minutes	
COOKING TIME: 1 hour 10 minutes	
MAKES: Approximately 450g/1lb	

3-4 thin-skinned oranges
280ml/½ pint white wine vinegar
340g/12oz sugar
1 cinnamon stick
2 whole allspice berries
4 whole cloves

Slice the oranges into 5mm/¼-inch rounds, discard the ends and pips. Place in a saucepan with enough water to cover. Simmer gently for about 40 minutes or until the peel is tender. Drain and discard the water. Heat the vinegar, sugar and spices in a shallow pan and add a layer of oranges. Simmer gently until the peel is transparent, remove and pack into sterilized jars. Repeat with all the orange slices. Boil the liquid for about 5 minutes until it starts to thicken. Pour over the fruit in the jars. Seal the jars and label.

Rum Fruit Compote

Traditionally fruits are added as they come into season.

PREPARATION TIME: 20 minutes	
MAKES: Approximately 2kg/4½lbs	

675g/1½lbs mixed fruits (Apples, pears,
*   peaches, plums, pineapples or cherries)*
450g/1lb brown sugar
Approximately 280ml/½ pint dark rum

Peel and quarter the apples and pears. Poach if under-ripe, for 3 minutes in a little water. Plunge the peaches in boiling water for a few seconds to

Right: Cherries and Peaches in Kirsch.

loosen the skin. Peel, then quarter and remove stones. Halve and stone the plums. Peel the pineapple, quarter, and core. Cut into 1.5cm/¾-inch thick chunks. Pack the fruit into jars, sprinkling each layer generously with sugar. Pour in enough rum to cover the fruit by about 1cm/

½ inch. Cover, label and store for at least 2 months in a cool, dark place.

Plums in Port

This makes a very sophisticated dessert.

PREPARATION TIME: 40 minutes

This page: Rum Fruit Compote.
Facing page: Brandied Apricots (top) and Spiced Orange Slices (bottom).

COOKING TIME: 40 minutes

MAKES: Approximately 1.8kg/4lbs

140ml/¼ pint water
225g/8oz sugar

280ml/½ pint ruby port
1.4kg/3lbs plums, halved and stoned
Few whole cloves

Heat the water and sugar, gently stirring until sugar dissolves, then boil for a few minutes. Remove from the heat and stir in the port. Pack the plums into jars and add 1 or 2 cloves to each jar. Pour in syrup to within 1cm/½ inch of the top of the jars. Add a little extra port if there is not enough syrup. Screw lids on then release a quarter turn. Place several layers of folded newspaper in the bottom of a deep pan. Put the jars in and fill the pan with water to the necks. Heat slowly in ½ hour to simmering. Simmer for 10 minutes. Turn off the heat, tighten the lids and allow to cool completely in the water. Label and store in a cool, dark place.

This page: Plums in Port.
Facing page: Grapes in Alsace Wine.

SWEET AND SAVOURY JELLIES

preserving pan and stir in the sugar. Heat gently until sugar dissolves. Boil rapidly for 5 minutes, then test for set. Boil for a few minutes longer if necessary, before testing again. Remove from the heat. Stir in the tarragon and allow to cool, stirring occasionally. When the jelly is on the point of setting stir in the grapes. Pour into sterilized jars. Make sure all the grapes are submerged in the jelly, then seal and label. Stores in the refrigerator for about 3 weeks.

Apple and Thyme Jelly

A savoury jelly which is delicious with cold pork or turkey.

PREPARATION TIME: 5 minutes

COOKING TIME: 10 minutes

MAKES: Approximately 900g/2lbs

850ml/1 ½ pints unsweetened clear apple juice
280ml/½ pint cider vinegar
675g/1 ½lbs sugar with added pectin
small handful fresh thyme leaves
Green food colouring (optional)

Pour the apple juice and vinegar into a preserving pan, bring to the boil and boil rapidly for 5 minutes. Stir in the sugar and heat until sugar dissolves. Add the thyme and boil rapidly for 5 minutes. Remove from the heat and test for a set, boil for a few minutes longer if required. Remove any scum and cool slightly and stir in food colouring if desired. Pour into hot, sterilized jars. Seal and label. Note: Other herbs such as basil, rosemary, marjoram, sage, or a mixture of several different herbs, may be used.

Grapes in Alsace Wine

A savoury jelly which makes an unusual accompaniment to poultry.

PREPARATION TIME: 5 minutes

COOKING TIME: 5 minutes

MAKES: Approximately 675g/1½lbs

75cl bottle Alsace wine such as
Gewurtztraminer or Riesling
15ml/1 tbsp white wine vinegar
450g/1lb sugar with added pectin
90g/3oz seedless green grapes
90g/3oz black grapes, halved and seeded
5ml/1 tsp dried tarragon or
15ml/1 tbsps fresh chopped tarragon

Pour the wine and vinegar into a

necessary, before testing again. Remove from the heat, skim away any scum. Allow to cool slightly, stirring until beginning to set, stir in the petals. Pour into sterilized jars. Seal and label.

Pawpaw (Papaya) Jelly

This pretty coloured, tasty jelly complements any meat.

PREPARATION TIME: 30 minutes, plus straining time

COOKING TIME: 30 minutes

MAKES: Approximately 675g/1½lbs

900g/2lbs pawpaw (papaya)
1 orange
15ml/1tbsp lemon juice
280ml/½ pint water
225g/8oz sugar with added pectin, for every 280ml/½ pint of juice

Wash the pawpaw, cut in half and discard the seeds. Cut the pawpaw into small pieces (do not peel) and place in a preserving pan. Chop the orange and add to the pan with the lemon juice and water. Cook until the fruit is soft and pulpy – about 20 minutes. Scald a jelly bag with boiling water and strain the fruit pulp through the bag suspended above a clean bowl. Leave to strain until the jelly bag stops dripping. Do not squeeze the bag. Measure the quantity of juice and add the sugar. Heat gently until sugar dissolves then boil rapidly for 5 minutes. Remove from the heat and test for a set, boil for a few minutes longer if required. Pour into hot, sterilized jars. Seal and label.

Chrysanthemum and Green Peppercorn Jelly

Nasturtium petals can be substituted in this exotic flavoured jelly which is delicious served with a grilled steak.

PREPARATION TIME: 5 minutes

COOKING TIME: 8 minutes

MAKES: Approximately 450g/1lb

570ml/1 pint unsweetened clear apple juice
340g/12oz sugar with added pectin
15ml/1 tbsp lemon juice
15ml/1 tbsp green peppercorns, packed in brine, well drained
Handful chrysanthemum petals, rinsed and dried

Pour the apple juice into a preserving pan and stir in the sugar and lemon juice. Heat gently until sugar dissolves. Add peppercorns and boil rapidly for 5 minutes, then test for set. Boil for a few minutes longer if

This page: Chrysanthemum and Green Peppercorn Jelly.
Facing page: Apple and Thyme Jelly (top) and Paw-Paw (Papaya) Jelly (bottom).

Port and Cranberry Jelly

Delicious with turkey, but too good to save for Christmas only.

PREPARATION TIME: 5 minutes
COOKING TIME: 15 minutes
MAKES: Approximately 900g/2lbs

570ml/1 pint ruby port

180g/6oz cranberries, washed
450g/1lb sugar with added pectin
1 bay leaf
15ml/1 tbsp lemon juice

Place the port and cranberries in a preserving pan and simmer gently for about 10 minutes or until the cranberries are tender. Stir in the

This page: Port and Cranberry Jelly. Facing page: Mint and Apple Jelly (top) and Apple Cider Jelly (bottom).

sugar, bay leaf and lemon juice. Heat gently until sugar dissolves. Bring to the boil and boil rapidly for 5 minutes, then test for setting by putting a spoonful onto a cold plate.

If the jelly forms a skin and wrinkles when the plate is tilted, the setting point has been reached. Boil for a few minutes longer if necessary, before testing again. Remove the bay leaf. Pour into hot, sterilized jars. Seal and label. Store in the refrigerator.

Spiced Tea Jelly

An unusual sweet jelly with a lovely spicy flavour.

PREPARATION TIME: 5 minutes, plus steeping time

COOKING TIME: 10 minutes

MAKES: Approximately 675g/1½lbs

1 orange
570ml/1 pint water
60ml/4 tbsps loose tea
1 cinnamon stick
4 whole cloves
1 allspice berry
340g/12oz sugar with added pectin

Pare the rind from the orange taking care not to include too much white pith. Place the orange rind, water, tea and spices in a pan and bring slowly to the boil. Once boiling, remove from the heat and allow to stand for 10 minutes. Strain through muslin and place in a preserving pan. Stir in the sugar and heat gently until sugar dissolves. Boil rapidly for 5 minutes. Remove from the heat and test for a set, boil for a few minutes longer if required. Pour into hot, sterilized jars. Seal and label.

Apple Cider Jelly

This delicious fruit jelly can be made at any time of the year.

PREPARATION TIME: 5 minutes

COOKING TIME: 8-10 minutes

MAKES: Approximately 675g/1½lbs

420ml/¾ pint dry cider
140ml/¼ pint clear unsweetened apple juice
450g/1lb sugar with added pectin

5ml/1 tsp lemon juice
1 cinnamon stick

Pour the cider and apple juice into a preserving pan and stir in the sugar and lemon juice. Add cinnamon stick. Heat gently until sugar dissolves. Bring to the boil and boil rapidly for 5 minutes, then test for set. Boil for a few minutes longer if necessary, before testing again. Remove cinnamon stick and pour into hot, sterilized jars. Seal and label.

Mint and Apple Jelly

Serve with roast lamb for a change to the traditional mint sauce.

PREPARATION TIME: 5 minutes

COOKING TIME: 15 minutes

MAKES: Approximately 675g/1½lbs

570ml/1 pint unsweetened clear apple juice
20ml/1½ tbsps cider vinegar
570ml/1 pint water
Small bunch mint, chopped
675g/1½lb sugar with added pectin

Place the apple juice, vinegar, water and half the mint in a preserving pan and bring to the boil. Boil for 5 minutes. Strain through a scalded jelly bag and return to the rinsed out pan. Stir in the sugar and heat gently until sugar dissolves. Boil rapidly for 5 minutes then test for set. Boil for a few minutes longer if necessary before testing again. Remove from the heat and stir in the remaining mint. Pour into hot, sterilized jars. Seal and label.

Peppered Grapefruit Jelly

This makes a tangy glaze for barbecued or grilled meat as well as providing a good accompaniment to duck and lamb.

PREPARATION TIME: 25 minutes

COOKING TIME: 30 minutes

MAKES: Approximately 450g/1lb

3 grapefruit
1 lemon
180g/6oz sugar, with added pectin, for every 280ml/½ pint juice
60ml/4 tbsps white rum
15ml/1 tbsp crushed peppercorns

Pare the rind from the grapefruit, taking care not to include too much white pith. Shred the peel finely. Squeeze the juice from the grapefruit and lemons, measure the quantity and pour into a preserving pan with an equal amount of water. Tie the pith and pips in a muslin bag and add to the pan. Add the grapefruit rind and cook for about 20 minutes or until the rind is soft. Remove the muslin bag and press out any juice, discard the bag. Measure the liquid, stir in the appropriate amount of sugar, and heat gently until sugar dissolves. Bring to the boil and boil rapidly for 5 minutes, then test for set. Boil for a few minutes longer if necessary, before testing again. Stir in the peppercorns and pour into hot, sterilized jars. Seal and label.

Beetroot and Chive Jelly

Serve this tangy jelly with salads as an alternative to pickled sliced vinegar.

PREPARATION TIME: 15 to 20 minutes

COOKING TIME: 1½ hours

MAKES: Approximately 450g/1lb

3 large uncooked beetroots
700 ml/1¼ pints water
140ml/¼ pint distilled malt vinegar
225g/8oz sugar with added pectin
45ml/3 tbsps snipped chives

Peel and slice the beetroot and place in a preserving pan. Add the water and cook for 1 hour or until the

Facing page: Spiced Tea Jelly (top) and Peppered Grapefruit Jelly (bottom).

beetroot is very soft. Push through a sieve, return to the pan and stir in the vinegar and sugar. Heat gently until sugar dissolves. Bring to the boil and boil rapidly until setting point is reached. Stir in the chives. Pour into hot, sterilized jars. Seal and label.

Guava and Lime Jelly

An exotic fruit jelly with a delicious tang.

PREPARATION TIME: 30 minutes

COOKING TIME: 40 minutes

MAKES: Approximately 450g/1lb

900g/2lbs guavas
3 limes
570ml/1 pint water
180g/6oz sugar, with added pectin, for
*   every 280ml/½ pint juice*

Wash and cut the guavas into chunks. Place in a preserving pan. Pare the rind from the limes, taking care not to include the white pith. Shred the rind finely, set aside. Squeeze the limes and add the juice to the pan with the water. Tie the pith and pips in a muslin bag and add to the pan. Cook for about 20 minutes or until the fruit is soft. Remove the muslin bag and press out any juice, discard the bag. Strain through a scalded jelly bag suspended above a clean bowl. Leave until the bag stops dripping and do not squeeze the bag. Measure the liquid, return to the pan and add the rind. Simmer for 10 to 15 minutes or until rind is softened, then stir in the appropriate amount of sugar and heat gently until sugar dissolves. Boil rapidly for 5 minutes then test for setting by putting a spoonful of jelly onto a cold plate. If the jelly forms a skin and wrinkles when the plate is tilted, the setting point has been reached. Boil for a few minutes longer if necessary, before testing again. Pour into hot, sterilized jars, then seal and label.

Guava and Lime Jelly (right) and Hot Pepper Jam (far right).

Strawberry and Pink Champagne Jelly

A sweet jelly that could be served as a dessert or a luxurious cake filling.

PREPARATION TIME: 5 minutes

COOKING TIME: 8 minutes

MAKES: Approximately 675g/1½lbs

75cl bottle pink champagne or rosé sparkling wine
450g/1lb sugar with added pectin
180g/6oz strawberries, hulled and halved

Put the champagne or wine and sugar in a preserving pan. Heat gently until sugar dissolves. Bring to the boil and boil rapidly for 5 minutes, then test for set. Boil for a few minutes longer if necessary, before testing again. Remove from the heat and allow to cool, stirring occasionally. When the jelly is on the point of setting stir in the strawberries. Pour into sterilized jars. Make sure all the fruit is submerged in the jelly, then seal and label. Stores in the refrigerator for about 3 weeks.

Hot Pepper Jelly

This savoury jelly will add a touch of spice to any barbecue or picnic.

PREPARATION TIME: 20 minutes

COOKING TIME: 10 minutes

MAKES: Approximately 900g/2lbs

3 red peppers, seeded
1 green pepper, seeded
2 red or green chillies, seeded
280ml/½ pint white wine vinegar
675g/1½lbs sugar with added pectin

Chop the peppers and chillies finely in a food processor or by hand. Place in a large saucepan or preserving pan, with the vinegar. Stir in the sugar and heat gently until sugar dissolves. Bring to the boil and boil rapidly for 5 minutes, then test for setting by putting a spoonful of jelly onto a cold plate. Leave for 2-3 minutes and if the jelly forms a skin and wrinkles when the plate is tilted, the setting point has been reached. Boil for a few minutes longer if necessary, before testing again. Pour into hot, sterilized jars. Seal and label.

This page: Beetroot and Chive Jelly. Facing page: Strawberry and Pink Champagne Jelly.

CHUTNEYS, PICKLES AND RELISHES

Pickled Orange Beetroots

Pickled beetroot with a delicious hint of orange and spice.

PREPARATION TIME: 15 minutes

COOKING TIME: 1-1½ hours

MAKES: Approximately 1.2kg/2¼lbs

900g/2lbs uncooked beetroots
Grated rind and juice of 2 oranges
180g/6oz sugar
1.1litre/2 pints distilled malt vinegar
2.5ml/½ tsp ground nutmeg

Wash the beetroot and cook in lightly salted boiling water for 1-1½ hours depending on their size. Peel the beetroot and slice and pack into jars. Place the orange rind, orange juice, sugar, vinegar and nutmeg in a saucepan and heat until boiling, stirring occasionally. Pour over the beetroot and seal immediately. Cool and label. Store in a cool, dark place.

Fennel Preserve with Aquavit

This highly-flavoured aniseed preserve makes an unusual accompaniment to cold meats.

PREPARATION TIME: 10 minutes

COOKING TIME: 15-20 minutes

MAKES: Approximately 900g/2lbs

3 heads of fennel
225g/8oz sugar
280ml/½ pint distilled malt vinegar
280ml/½ pint water
Pinch salt
15ml/1 tbsp caraway seeds

140ml/¼ pint aquavit

Cut the root ends off the fennel and cut fennel into 1cm/½ inch slices. Include the green tops. Place the sugar, vinegar, water, salt and caraway seeds in a large saucepan and heat

This page: Pickled Orange Beetroots.
Facing page: Fennel Preserve with Aquavit (top) and Pickled Carrots and Walnuts (bottom).

gently. Stir until sugar dissolves and boil for 5 minutes. Add the sliced fennel and cook for 10 minutes or until the fennel looks translucent. Stir in the aquavit. Pour into hot, sterilized jars. Seal and label.

Pickled Carrots and Walnuts

Serve as part of a mixed hors d'oeuvres or with cold meats.

PREPARATION TIME: 15 minutes

COOKING TIME: 35 minutes

MAKES: Approximately 1.2kg/2¼lbs

900g/2lbs carrots
280ml/½ pint cider vinegar
450g/1lb sugar
1.25ml/¼ tsp ground nutmeg
1.25ml/¼ tsp ground ginger
2 whole cloves
120g/4oz walnut halves

Peel the carrots and chop roughly, then blanch in lightly salted boiling water for 5 minutes; the carrots should still be crisp. Drain and reserve 600ml/1pint of the water. Pour the reserved water into a large saucepan and stir in the vinegar, sugar and spices. Bring to the boil and boil rapidly for 10 minutes or until reduced by a quarter. Add the carrots and walnuts and cook for a further 15-20 minutes or until the carrots look translucent. Pour into hot, sterilized jars. Seal and label.

Sweet and Sour Onions

Nothing quite beats the crunch of home-made pickled onions, perfect for picnics or salads.

PREPARATION TIME: 20 minutes

COOKING TIME: 1 hour

MAKES: Approximately 1.8kg/4lbs

1.4kg/3lbs button or pickling onions
850ml/1½ pints cider vinegar
340g/12oz light brown sugar
30ml/2 tbsps mustard seeds
1 cinnamon stick
5ml/1 tsp salt

Pour boiling water over the onions to loosen the skins and then peel. Bring a large pan of water to the boil and add a couple of tablespoons of the vinegar; blanch the onions for 5 minutes. Drain and pat dry. Pack into preserving jars. Heat the remaining ingredients together until boiling and pour over the onions to within 1cm/½ inch of the top of the jar. Screw the lids onto the jars then release a quarter turn. Place several layers of folded newspaper in the bottom of a pan which is deep enough to fill with warm water to the tops of the jars. Place the jars in the pan. Fill the pan with water up to the necks of the jars and heat slowly to simmering point; this should take about 30 minutes. Maintain the water at simmering point for 10 minutes. Turn off the heat, tighten the lids and allow the jars to cool completely in the water. Label and store in a cool, dark place.

Pepper Relish

A lightly spiced relish perfect on hamburgers or with any barbecued food.

PREPARATION TIME: 20 minutes

COOKING TIME: 40 minutes

MAKES: Approximately 675g/1½lbs

2 red peppers, seeded
2 green peppers, seeded
2 yellow peppers, seeded
1 large onion, peeled and chopped
1.25ml/¼ tsp dried tarragon
1.25ml/¼ tsp ground cloves
5ml/1 tsp celery seasoning
340g/12oz sugar
570ml/1 pint distilled malt vinegar

Slice the peppers, then cut into dice.

Right: Sweet and Sour Onions.

Place the onion, tarragon, cloves, celery seasoning, sugar and vinegar in a large saucepan or preserving pan and heat, stirring until sugar dissolves. Add the peppers and boil rapidly for about 35 minutes. The mixture should thicken instantly when spooned onto a cold plate. Pour into hot, sterilized jars. Seal and label.

Chinese Corn Pickles

An unusual addition to a mixed hors d'oeuvres tray or cold table.

PREPARATION TIME: 15 minutes

COOKING TIME: 18 minutes

MAKES: Approximately 1.4kg/3lbs

340g/12oz baby corn

3 red chillies, seeded and cut into thin strips
5cm/2inch piece root ginger, peeled and cut into thin strips
2 pieces star anise
10ml/1 tbsp soy sauce
90ml/6 tbsps sherry
90ml/6 tbsps sugar
5ml/1 tsp salt
420ml/¾ pint rice vinegar or white malt vinegar

Cook the baby corn in boiling water until just tender, but still crisp. Drain well and pack into jars. Place the chillies, ginger, anise, soy, sherry, sugar, salt and vinegar in a pan and heat, stirring, until sugar dissolves. Bring to the boil then pour over the baby corn. Seal and label. Best stored in the refrigerator.

Green Tomato Relish

This recipe is an ideal way to use up those tomatoes which refuse to ripen fully.

PREPARATION TIME: 20 minutes

COOKING TIME: 40 minutes

MAKES: Approximately 1.2kg/2¼lbs

1.2kg/2¼lbs green tomatoes
3 small onions, peeled and chopped
90g/3oz currants
1.25ml/¼ tsp ground ginger
1.25ml/¼ tsp mustard seeds
280ml/½ pint cider vinegar
150g/5oz light brown sugar
Salt and pepper

Plunge the tomatoes into boiling water for a few seconds, remove and peel. Cut into dice. Place in a large saucepan with the onion, currants, ginger, mustard seeds and vinegar. Bring to the boil then simmer for 15 minutes. Stir in the sugar and season with salt and pepper. Cook gently, stirring until sugar dissolves, then increase the heat and boil rapidly until the mixture is thick and leaves a trail

This page: Chinese Corn Pickles. Facing page: Green Tomato Relish (top) and Pepper Relish (bottom).

when a wooden spoon is pulled through it. This should take about 15 minutes. Pour into hot, sterilized jars. Seal and label. Best stored in the refrigerator.

Curried Fruit

This pickle is very quick to make and goes particularly well with cold pork.

PREPARATION TIME: 15 minutes

COOKING TIME: 15 minutes

MAKES: Approximately 1.2kg/2¼lbs

225g/8oz light brown sugar
140ml/¼ pint distilled malt vinegar
140ml/¼ pint water
4 whole cloves
30ml/2 tbsps mild curry powder
5ml/1 tsp coriander seeds

This page: Curried Fruits.
Facing page: Apple and Fig Chutney (top) and Pineapple, Mango and Mint Chutney (bottom).

3 apples, peeled, cored and thickly sliced
180g/6oz pineapple chunks
90g/3oz raisins
6 apricots, stoned and halved

Place the sugar, vinegar, water, cloves, curry powder and coriander seeds in a large saucepan or preserving pan and heat gently, stirring until sugar dissolves. Boil for 2 minutes. Add the apples, pineapple and raisins and cook for 5 minutes, add the apricots and cook for another 3 minutes. The apple should look translucent. Pour into hot, sterilized jars, then seal and label. After opening store in the refrigerator.

Piccalilli

A traditional English pickle. Any vegetables that are surplus or cheap can be used, but this combination works well.

PREPARATION TIME: 20 minutes, plus 6 hours standing time

COOKING TIME: 15-20 minutes

MAKES: Approximately 1.1kg/2¼lbs

340g/12oz pickling cucumbers, diced
340g/12oz onions, peeled and chopped
340g/12oz cauliflower, cut into small florets
1 large green pepper, seeded and diced
Salt
280ml/½ pint distilled malt vinegar
15-30ml/1-2 tbsps yellow mustard
2.5ml/½ tsp turmeric
2.5ml/½ tsp mustard seeds
1.25ml/¼ tsp dried thyme
1 bay leaf
60g/2oz sugar
15ml/1 tbsp cornflour mixed with a little water

Layer the vegetables in a dish, sprinkle each layer liberally with salt, and leave for at least 6 hours to draw out water from the vegetables. Rinse and drain well. Place the vegetables in a large saucepan or preserving pan and add the vinegar, mustard, turmeric, mustard seeds, thyme, bay leaf and sugar. Stir to mix well. Bring gently to the boil and simmer for 8 minutes until the vegetables are cooked but still crisp. Stir in the cornflour mixture and cook until thickened. Pour into hot, sterilized jars, then seal and label.

Red and White Radish Preserve

A colourful sweet relish for hors d'eourves or the buffet table.

PREPARATION TIME: 10 minutes

COOKING TIME: 15 minutes

MAKES: Approximately 450g/1lb

180g/6oz red radishes
180g/6oz white radishes (sometimes known as mooli or daikon radish)
570ml/1 pint clear honey
15ml/1 tbsp lemon juice
15ml/1 tbsp grated root ginger
90g/3oz Brazil nuts, roughly chopped

Cut the radishes into 5mm/¼ inch slices. Cook in lightly salted boiling water for 5 minutes or until just tender. Drain and mix with the remaining ingredients and cook gently for 10 minutes, until all the flavours are combined. Pour into hot, sterilized jars, then seal and label. Best stored in the refrigerator.

Apple and Fig Chutney

A fabulous pickle which, by using dried figs, can be made at any time of the year.

PREPARATION TIME: 35 minutes

COOKING TIME: 30 minutes

MAKES: Approximately 1.8kg/4lbs

900g/2lbs apples, such as Bramley or Granny Smith
450g/1lb dried or fresh figs
3 small onions, peeled and chopped
120g/4oz raisins
850ml/1½ pints white wine vinegar
15ml/1 tbsp coriander seeds, lightly crushed
5ml/1 tsp ground ginger
2.5ml/½ tsp cayenne pepper
2.5ml/½ tsp salt
570g/1¼lbs light brown sugar

Peel, core and roughly chop the apples, and chop the figs. Place in a preserving pan with the onions, raisins, vinegar, coriander, ginger, cayenne and salt. Cook for 15 minutes until the apples are soft and mushy. Stir in the sugar and heat gently until sugar dissolves, then boil rapidly until thickened, stirring frequently to prevent it from burning on the bottom of the pan. Test by stirring with a wooden spoon, if the spoon leaves a channel then the mixture is ready. Pour into hot, sterilized jars, then seal and label.

Pineapple, Mango and Mint Chutney

An exotic sweet pickle, the flavour goes excellently with a strong Cheddar cheese.

PREPARATION TIME: 20 minutes, plus several hours standing time

COOKING TIME: 35 minutes

MAKES: Approximately 1.4kg/3lbs

1 large pineapple
Salt
2 large mangoes, peeled, stoned and chopped
225g/8oz sultanas
850ml/1½ pint distilled white vinegar
45ml/3 tbsps chopped fresh mint
15ml/1 tbsp chopped ginger root
2.5ml/½ tsp ground nutmeg
450g/1lb sugar

Peel the pineapple and chop. Layer in a shallow dish, sprinkle liberally with salt and leave for several hours, or overnight. Rinse pineapple and drain well. Place the pineapple, mango, sultanas, vinegar, mint, ginger and nutmeg in a preserving pan and simmer gently for 10 minutes until the fruits are tender. Stir in the sugar and heat gently until sugar dissolves, then boil rapidly until thickened, stirring

Facing page: Red and White Radish Preserve (top) and Piccalilli (bottom).

sugar in a preserving pan and cook gently for 20-30 minutes until the pumpkin is tender. Stir in the sugar and heat gently until it dissolves, then boil rapidly until thickened, stirring frequently to prevent it from burning on the bottom of the pan. Test by stirring with a wooden spoon; if the spoon leaves a channel then the mixture is ready. Pour into hot, sterilized jars, then seal and label.

Bread and Butter Pickle

A simple, attractive pickle. Serve with fish or cold meats.

PREPARATION TIME: 15 minutes, plus several hours standing time

COOKING TIME: 10 minutes

MAKES: Approximately 1.2kg/2¼lbs

675g/1½lbs pickling cucumbers
Salt
570ml/1 pint distilled malt vinegar
450g/1lb sugar
30ml/2 tbsps mustard seeds
1.25ml/¼ tsp turmeric
Pinch cayenne pepper

Slice the cucumbers and place in a shallow dish, sprinkle liberally with salt and leave for several hours. Drain and rinse well. Place the remaining ingredients in a large pan and bring to the boil, stirring well. Boil for 2-3 minutes, add the sliced cucumber and boil for 5 minutes or until the cucumber looks translucent. Pour into hot, sterilized jars, then seal and label.

frequently to prevent it from burning on the bottom of the pan. Test by stirring with a wooden spoon, if the spoon leaves a channel then the mixture is ready. Pour into hot, sterilized jars, then seal and label.

Pumpkin Chutney

A chunky pickle, delicious served with a ploughman's lunch.

PREPARATION TIME: 20 minutes

COOKING TIME: 45 minutes

MAKES: Approximately 1.8kg/4lbs

This page: Pumpkin Chutney. Facing page: Bread and Butter Pickle (top) and Tarragon Vinegar Pickle (bottom).

1.4kg/3lbs pumpkin flesh, small diced
2 lemons, thinly sliced
30ml/2 tbsps grated root ginger
340g/12oz raisins
700ml/1¼ pint water
570ml/1 pint white wine vinegar
900g/2lbs light brown sugar

Place all the ingredients except the

Tarragon Vinegar Pickle

Serve in a mixed hors d'oeuvres or with any fish, hot or cold.

PREPARATION TIME: 10 minutes, plus several hours standing time

COOKING TIME: 15-20 minutes

MAKES: Approximately 900g/2lbs

675g/1½lbs pickling cucumbers
Salt

420ml/¾ pint white wine vinegar
140ml/¼ pint water
225g/8oz sugar
1 bunch tarragon, chopped
5 black peppercorns

Cut the cucumbers in half, if large, and then into quarters lengthwise. Place in a shallow dish, sprinkle liberally with salt and leave for several hours. Drain and rinse well. Place the remaining ingredients in a large pan and bring to the boil, stirring well. Boil for 2-3 minutes, add the sliced cucumber and boil for 10 minutes or until they lose their bright green colour. Pour into hot, sterilized jars, then seal and label.

Watermelon and Lime Pickle

Serve this unusual pickle with an Indian meal, perfect with poppadoms.

PREPARATION TIME: 20 minutes, plus overnight standing

COOKING TIME: 30-35 minutes

MAKES: Approximately 450g/1lb

675g/1½lbs watermelon rind
Salt
4 limes
280ml/½ pint distilled malt vinegar
340g/12oz sugar
1 stick cinnamon
2 whole cloves

Peel off the dark green skin from the watermelon rind and scrape off any remaining flesh. Cut the rind into 2.5cm/1inch squares. Place in a shallow dish and sprinkle liberally with salt. Leave to stand for 12 hours or overnight. Rinse and drain well. Thinly slice two of the limes and squeeze the juice from the remaining two. Combine the lime juice, vinegar, sugar and spices in a preserving pan and bring to the boil. Boil for 5 minutes, then remove the spices. Add the prepared melon rind and cook for 15 minutes or until the rind begins to look translucent. Add the lime slices and cook for a further 10 minutes. Pour into

hot, sterilized jars, then seal and label.

Spicy Cantaloupe Pickle

Serve with cold meats or curries.

PREPARATION TIME: 30 minutes

COOKING TIME: 15 minutes, plus 3 hours standing time

MAKES: Approximately 1.4kg/3lbs

2 cantaloupe melons, slightly under-ripe
340g/12oz sugar
420ml/¾ pint distilled malt vinegar
140ml/¼ pint water
4 whole cloves
1 stick cinnamon

Cut the melon in half and scoop out the seeds. Cut into quarters and remove the rind. Cut the melon into 2.5cm/1inch chunks. Mix together

**This page: Corn Relish.
Facing Page: Watermelon and Lime Pickle (top) and Spicy Cantaloupe Pickle (bottom).**

the remaining ingredients in a preserving pan or large saucepan. Bring gently to the boil, stirring until the sugar dissolves. Boil for 5 minutes. Remove from the heat, stir in the melon and leave for 3 hours. Return to the heat and bring slowly back up to the boil. Boil for 5 minutes. Pour into hot, sterilized jars, then seal and label. Best stored in the refrigerator.

Corn Relish

Popular for barbecues, this relish is delicious on sausages and hamburgers.

PREPARATION TIME: 20 minutes

COOKING TIME: 35 minutes

MAKES: Approximately 1.2g/2¼lbs

180g/6oz celery, chopped
1 onion, peeled and chopped
7.5ml/¾ tbsp celery seasoning
5ml/1 tsp mustard seed
1.25ml/¼ tsp turmeric
15ml/1 tbsp cornflour
300ml/12 fl oz distilled malt vinegar
200ml/7 fl oz water
340g/12oz sweetcorn niblets, fresh or frozen
2 red peppers, seeded and diced
120g/4oz sugar

Place the celery, onion, celery seasoning, mustard seeds, turmeric and cornflour in a large saucepan and gradually stir in the vinegar and water. Bring gently to the boil and cook for 5 minutes, stir in the remaining ingredients and cook slowly for 25 minutes until the mixture is very thick and the vegetables are tender. Pour into hot, sterilized jars, then seal and label.

Chilli Sauce

Use in place of your usual ketchup for a sauce with a bit more bite.

PREPARATION TIME: 20 minutes

COOKING TIME: 35 minutes

MAKES: Approximately 1.8kg/4lbs

675g/1½lb tomatoes
3 large onions, peeled and chopped
2 green peppers, seeded and diced
2 red chillies, seeded and chopped
280ml/½ pint cider vinegar
5ml/1 tsp mustard seeds
5ml/1 tsp celery seasoning
2.5ml/½ tsp chilli powder
1.25ml/¼ tsp ground cloves
1.25ml/¼ tsp ground cinnamon
Pinch ground allspice
1 bay leaf
180g/6oz brown sugar

Plunge the tomatoes into boiling water for a few seconds to loosen their skins. Skin and chop the tomatoes. Put all the ingredients except the sugar in

a preserving pan, bring gently to the boil, stirring, and cook until all the vegetables are soft. Stir in the sugar and continue cooking until the mixture is thick and a wooden spoon leaves a trail when pulled through it. Remove the bay leaf and pour into hot, sterilized jars. Seal and label.

Cranberry Orange Relish

A sweet pickle that goes well with poultry.

PREPARATION TIME: 10 minutes

COOKING TIME: 20 minutes

MAKES: Approximately 900g/2lb

This page: Cranberry Orange Relish. Facing page: Chilli Sauce (top) and Mincemeat (bottom).

3 small oranges
675g/1½lbs cranberries
150g/5oz sugar
2.5ml/½ tsp ground allspice
200ml/7 fl oz red wine
15ml/1 tbsp red wine vinegar
  (optional)

Pare the rind from the orange, taking care not to include too much white pith. Squeeze the juice from the

Pinch salt
225g/8oz whole dried fruit, such as
    prunes, apricots, peaches, pears,
    apples and figs
225g/8oz glacé fruits, such as cherries,
    lemon and orange peel and pineapple

Place the sugar, mustard powder, mustard seeds, water, vinegar and salt in a large saucepan and bring to the boil, stirring. Add all the dried and glacé fruit, stir well. Cover and leave to stand for at least 4 hours. Return to the heat and bring gently to the boil; simmer for 10 minutes. Pour into hot, sterilized jars, then seal and label. Store in the refrigerator after opening.

Mincemeat

Once you have made this recipe you will not buy ready-made mincemeat again.

PREPARATION TIME: 25 minutes	
COOKING TIME: 15 minutes	
MAKES: Approximately 1.8kg/4lbs	

900g/2lbs apples, peeled, cored and
    finely chopped
275g/10oz raisins
225g/8oz suet
120g/4oz chopped mixed peel
Grated rind and juice of 1 orange
200ml/7 fl oz water
10ml/2 tsp ground cinnamon
2.5ml/½ tsp ground nutmeg
2.5ml/½ tsp ground cloves
1.25ml/¼ tsp ground ginger
120g/4oz dark brown sugar
60ml/4 tbsps dark rum or brandy

Place all the ingredients except the sugar and rum or brandy, in a preserving pan. Cook gently on a very low heat for 10 minutes until all the flavours are well combined and the apple is just soft, but not mushy. Stir in the sugar and cook for a further 5 minutes, then stir in the rum or brandy. Pack into hot, sterilized jars, then seal and label. Store in a cool, dark place.

This page: Mustard Fruit.
Facing page: Lemon Vinegar (top)
and Garlic Vinegar (bottom).

oranges. Chop the rind very finely in a food processor, add the cranberries and process briefly. Place the sugar, orange juice and allspice in a preserving pan and cook gently until sugar dissolves. Add the cranberries, orange rind and wine. Cook gently until the cranberries are tender and the mixture is very thick, stirring frequently. Taste and add the wine vinegar if the relish is too sweet. Pour into hot, sterilized jars, then seal and label. Best stored in the refrigerator.

Mustard Fruit

An unusual accompaniment to cold meats, it makes an attractive addition to a buffet table.

PREPARATION TIME: 15 minutes, plus 4 hours standing time	
COOKING TIME: 25 to 30 minutes	
MAKES: Approximately 675g/1½lbs	

340g/12oz sugar
22.5ml/1½ tbsps mustard powder
10ml/2 tsps mustard seeds
700ml/1¼ pints water
140ml/¼ pint white wine vinegar

FLAVOURED SYRUPS AND VINEGARS

Garlic Vinegar

Use to give a hint of garlic to salad dressings.

PREPARATION TIME: 5 minutes

COOKING TIME: 5 minutes

MAKES: 350ml/12.3 fl oz

350ml/12.3 fl oz bottle of cider vinegar
3 cloves garlic, peeled
1 bay leaf

Pour the vinegar into a saucepan and heat to simmering point. Thread the garlic onto a skewer and put this into the bottle along with the bay leaf. Return the warm vinegar to the bottle and seal immediately. Label and store in a cool, dark place for 2 weeks before using. Keeps 2 months.

Raspberry Syrup

Dilute with milk or water for a delicious drink or as a sauce for desserts.

PREPARATION TIME: 30 minutes

COOKING TIME: 1 hour 20 minutes

MAKES: Approximately 570ml/1 pint

900g/2lbs raspberries, fresh or frozen
340g/12oz sugar
200ml/7 fl oz water
Half a cinnamon stick
15ml/1 tbsp lemon juice
60ml/4 tbsps raspberry liqueur (optional)

Cook the raspberries for 5-10 minutes until they break up, then push through a sieve. Place the raspberry juice, sugar, water, cinnamon and lemon juice in a pan and bring to the boil; simmer gently for 30 minutes. Strain through muslin. Stir in liqueur if using and pour into screw-top bottles or jars. Seal, then release the lids a quarter turn. Place the bottles in a pan lined with a few sheets of newspaper and add enough cold water to come up to the caps. Bring very slowly to simmering point and simmer for 30 minutes. Remove bottles, tighten the lids and allow to

immediately . Label and store in a cool, dark place for 2 weeks before using. Keeps 2 months.

Cherry Vinegar

A perfect gift for a 'foodie' friend or relative.

PREPARATION TIME: 5 minutes	
COOKING TIME: 5 minutes	
MAKES: Approximately 350ml/12 fl oz	

90g/3oz red or black cherries, stems left on
280ml/½ pint distilled malt vinegar
Pinch sugar

Place all the ingredients in a saucepan and heat gently to simmering point. If the cherries do not colour the vinegar crush against the side of the pan and simmer for 1 to 2 minutes. Pour the cherries and vinegar into a bottle whilst still warm. Seal, label and store for 2 weeks before using. Keeps 2 months.

Lemon Vinegar

Perfect for a salad dressing or sprinkled on grilled or fried fish.

PREPARATION TIME: 5 minutes	
COOKING TIME: 5 minutes	
MAKES: 350ml/12fl oz	

1 lemon
280ml/½ pint distilled malt vinegar
2.5ml/½ tsp sugar

Pare the rind from the lemon, taking care not to include too much white pith. Shred the rind finely and squeeze the juice. Heat the lemon juice, vinegar and sugar together in a pan until simmering point. Push the lemon rind into a bottle and pour on the warm vinegar, seal immediately. Label and store for 2 weeks before using. Keeps 2 months.

This page: Blueberry Syrup (top) and Raspberry Syrup (bottom). Facing page: Cherry Vinegar (top) and Rosemary Vinegar (bottom).

cool. Label and store in a cool, dark place.

Blueberry Syrup

Blueberry syrup makes a delicious sauce for vanilla ice cream or can be used to make a refreshing drink.

PREPARATION TIME: 20 minutes	
COOKING TIME: 1 hour 35 minutes	
MAKES: Approximately 570ml/1 pint	

675g/1½lbs blueberries, fresh or frozen
140ml/¼ pint water
15ml/1 tbsp lemon juice
340g/12oz sugar
60ml/4 tbsps crème de cassis (optional)

Cook the blueberries in the water and lemon juice for 45 minutes, crushing against the side of the pan occasionally. Strain through a scalded jelly bag. Return the juice to the pan and add the sugar. Heat gently, stirring, until sugar dissolves. Boil for 5 minutes. Stir in liqueur if using and pour into screw-top bottles or jars.

Seal, then release the lids a quarter turn. Place the bottles in a pan lined with a few sheets of newspaper and add enough cold water to come up to the caps. Bring very slowly to simmering point and simmer for 30 minutes. Remove bottles, tighten the lids and allow to cool. Label and store in a cool, dark place.

Rosemary Vinegar

Use to add extra flavour to home-made pickles and chutneys or salad dressings.

PREPARATION TIME: 5 minutes	
COOKING TIME: 5 minutes	
MAKES: 350ml/12.3 fl oz	

350ml/12.3 fl oz bottle red wine vinegar
6 sprigs fresh rosemary
3 black peppercorns

Pour the vinegar into a saucepan and heat to simmering point. Wash and dry the rosemary, push into the bottle with the peppercorns. Return the warm vinegar to the bottle and seal

INDEX